Digging for Gold

[in the rule]

LWS
BOOKS
©2006

DIGGING

FOR

GOLD

[in the rule]

Jonathan Richard Cring

LWS Books
P.O. Box 833
Hendersonville, TN 37077-0833
(800) 643-4718 ext. 74
lwsbooks.com

LWS Books are available at special quantity discounts for
bulk purchases for sales promotions, premiums, fund-
raising, and educational needs. Special books or book
excerpts also can be created to fit specific needs.
For details, write: LWS Books Special Markets,
P.O. Box 833, Hendersonville, TN 37077

ISBN 978-0-9704361-6-0

Library of Congress Control Number: 2005907938

For information on the authors touring schedule visit:
WWW.JANETHAN.COM

Cover Design by Angela Cring, Clazzy Studios

Manufactured and Printed in the United States

Preface

It started with one shopping cart being discarded by one very busy man, wearing a burgundy beret. He left it in the middle of a parking space and ran off to his car. The next lady, seeing the cart in the space, added hers to it and scurried away. Still another gentleman, rationalizing in his own mind that it was the "new place to put carts," stacked his on to the other two—a train of three. This last man happened to jiggle the arrangement to the extent that the trio of carts wobbled onto the parking lot into a lane of traffic. A man driving by, nearly hitting the moving three, got out of his car and, in a fit of anger, shoved them to the side. They careened and collided into the side of a car, where a woman was placing her crying child at that moment. This surprise jolt caused the young one to wail louder. The mother screamed at her son, slapped him, pushed the carts away, checked for damage and got into her car and jerked away, barely missing a teenager on a bike, who gave her the finger.

Meanwhile the carts were rolling, stopped for a moment by another man who inserted his own into the collage and strolled away. Then a fifth woman attached her cart to the collection, but her dress got caught. She yanked to free herself and as she whirled, the five grocery buggies went speeding toward the street. She thought about chasing them, but her dress was torn and she was late.

The carts gained momentum down an incline and rolled onto the main street into traffic in front of a transit bus that swerved to miss them, striking the car in the opposite lane. It was a direct hit, and the man inside was not wearing a seat belt, just a burgundy beret. He was pronounced dead at the scene.

Do unto others . . . it all does make a difference.

Sitting One

She was seventeen, maybe sixteen—difficult to pinpoint age in a woman, especially a young woman. She was a waitress, doing a respectable job if you can ascertain such things by the fact that she brought water and made sure we had silverware. I had just placed my order—meatloaf—a treat you occasionally require and only at a restaurant when you get in a particular mood to want something specific, like, ah . . . meatloaf. It couldn't have been more than two minutes until she was back at my table again, a little nervous. (My experience was telling me that I was about to be disappointed.)

"I'm sorry," she said sweetly. "Our cook did not make meatloaf today. But we are offering a delicious substitute." (The word "delicious" was certainly decreed by an overly-zealous manager.)

I smiled and said, "O.K. What is the substitute?"

"Baked chicken," she piped, smile affixed.

Not a reasonable facsimile. Call me fussy, but chicken is not a replacement for meatloaf. Meatloaf generally comes from a cow or a pig or some delightful union of the pair, while chickens have feathers and cluck. I do not think because they are both from the barnyard, that they are equivalent or a reasonable stand-in for each other.

I giggled.

She was a little offended. "Well, I can always give you grilled cheese." This one made me laugh out loud. Grilled cheese seemed even further away from meat loaf than baked chicken.

I asked her if she could give me grilled chicken and then grind it and press it into a loaf. She didn't think I was funny.

This brings me to my point. Things aren't the same unless they're the same, and if they're not the same then they are different.

Duh.

I was listening to some preacher on television. He told me to "love my neighbor as myself" *and* to "do unto others as you would have them do unto you." This fine chap seemed to think the two thoughts were synonymous. He seemed to think that both of these fell under the broad context of being different wordings of the golden rule.

I don't think so.

Truthfully, I think only one of these is the golden rule, and the other one is just "what is." What I mean is that the other one is the status quo.

Honestly, I think everybody, directly or indirectly, loves their neighbor as themselves. The problem is, too often we are all just inundated with so much self-deception that we think we have the right to cheat and lie to everybody else. We are obsessed with so much insecurity that we can't possibly trust anyone else. And we are hounded by a considerable amount of self-loathing, which causes us to treat people with every approach ranging from indifference to contempt.

I know the popular belief is that people really love themselves.

But I think when you have a heart, a mind and a soul living within the confines of the same container of skin, the three of them find it very difficult to convince each other that everything is peaches and cream, when it just doesn't feel sweet and fruity. I think it works this way: the minute you get the mind calmed down into thinking everything is all right, the heart and the emotions rise up and demand equal attention, as the soul sits back quietly, trying to be as inconspicuous as possible, for fear that it is going to be yelled at again and told to "shut up and stay out of this."

Living in this flesh and blood soap opera causes us to be a bit tentative— bouncing between self-incriminating or self-righteous when we least need to be so. Yes, I do believe we probably love other people about as much as we care about ourselves. Trouble is, we live in an identity crisis casting a shadow over any generosity we might extend to our fellow man, often causing us to portray a sense of impending doom.

Now, on the other hand, "do unto others as you would have them do unto you" is a cleansing act of faith launching us from our perch of mediocrity to higher realms of concern and hope. With DUO (*do unto others*) I'm figuring out what I really need to have done to myself—the dream human makeover—and providing that same vision of spirit to my fellow traveler.

But the trouble with all ideas is that they're just ideas until they get plugged into a plan of action.

So if "love thy neighbor as thyself" is the condition and "do unto others" is the cure, what is the treatment to set the process in motion?

You gotta go for the gold, if you can dig it.

Gold just doesn't float in the air. You gotta pan for it, or you gotta get a shovel. Digging for gold means going through an awful lot of solid rock to find a few glowing embers.

By the way, I ordered the liver and onions.

She came back two minutes later and told me they were out of onions. I decided it was a day to fast.

Sitting Two

He was almost eighteen years old, and I was sensing some sort of primitive tribal urge to pass on my stories to him before he left the home fires in search of his own burning flame. He was blond, about six feet tall, 170 pounds, handsome and president of his high school student body.

He was my son.

I wanted to say something profound to him. So I went on a drive, hoping to share a series of tales about my life, in a quest to get him to understand his dad's journey and choices. Anticipating there might be a slight boredom factor, I had intelligently purchased an array of burgers, fries, condiments and dairy confections to encourage wakefulness and attention.

I didn't know where to start.

I really don't care what my children grow up to be or even what their preferences are. I just really would like them to be decent folk who give a damn about other people. Actually, maybe that's the hardest thing to teach anyone.

I just started telling him stories.

When my wife, Dollie, and I got married, we had two kids quicker than you can say "you need to go get birth control." Oops. The first one was Jon Russell and the second was Joshua Paul. We were very young, filled with energy and saturated with dreams. Neither of us was gainfully employed, and as you probably know, the exchange rate on dreams to dollars is very low.

We earned a few bucks here and there picking blackberries and selling them door to door and by singing in an occasional coffeehouse, where the patrons would squeeze out a little change. We moved into an apartment—rent, an amazing $50 a month. Amazing to me now because of how ridiculously inexpensive it was. Amazing then because $50 was five hundred dimes.

We were able to buy bologna and bread but not to pay the landlord's request.

We also had an additional problem. Our little apartment should never have been rented to us because it was already occupied. I suppose the landlord didn't like these occupants any better than us, because they, too, were non rent-payers.

They were cockroaches. I don't like the word. To this day, a chill goes down my spine when I speak it aloud. We didn't just have a few cockroaches. Our apartment was not just infested by a nest. Dollie and I had happened upon the breeding headquarters for Cockroach, International—a work in progress. We had cockroaches of every size, color, ethnic origin, religious orientation, and, dare I say, sexual preference.

Our little hovel was so riddled with cockroaches that we even had a small albino colony that lived off by itself in the darker region of a closet so as not to risk exposure to the light.

We had a dilemma. It's difficult to ask your landlord to remove the cockroach colony when you are trying to avoid the same landlord because you can't pay your rent.

So we tried every possible home remedy. I tried Raid. They were drawn to the fragrance, refreshed. I tried the roach motels. They would fill them up, double book, share rooms, but there always seemed to be plenty more patrons. I tried killing them with my bare hands. Not only did this freak me out, but also it was an act of futility because I think they felt like it was some sort of masochistic game of tag.

We tried to live with them. There is a reason that roaches have been around for millions of years, and ours made it clear to us that they had no intention of peaceful co-existence, nor of honoring any of our space—even our personal body space.

Now, the reason I tell you this story is not to gross you out and most definitely not to make myself look good. It's just to let you know what we finally had to decide.

Sometimes, the cockroaches win.

Sometimes, the vermin can't be eradicated by extermination plans. Sometimes the pests that exist feed off the goodness around them and turn it into nasty waste.

Sometimes, even things that were intended to be good, like having a home, become so overwhelmed by the creeping, crawling crud, that the only solution is to abandon the site.

Dollie and I had to come to the conclusion that the cockroaches may not be smarter than us; nor be bigger than us, and they may not be more powerful than us, but they certainly were more plentiful.

Sometimes, when we're digging for gold in the rule, trying to "do unto others as you would have them do unto you," we run across a nest of cockroaches, determined to maintain their status, and so abundant that any attempts to eradicate them will leave us frustrated, unfulfilled.

If I cannot identify the nasty enemies of goodwill, friendship and brotherhood, I may be in danger of beginning to believe that ideals like the golden rule are merely dreams of a vagabond carpenter turned preacher who lost contact with reality.

Sometimes, the cockroaches win. Dollie and I had to move out of the apartment to be free of cockroaches. Actually, we had to burn most of our furniture and clothes because they were infiltrated with the little hairy-legged crawlers and their eggs.

It was a debilitating time, but shortcuts would only have kept the cockroaches close.

Sometimes, the cockroaches win. But we should learn to recognize what breeds them and what welcomes them into the sanctity of our homes.

So what are the cockroaches that eat away at the gold? What is the social slime that discourages us from the pursuit of digging for gold in the rule?

Sitting Three

The breeding ground for human struggle leading to dissent is religion. The cockroaches, creeping from the birthing pod—fundamentalists. Every war, all strife, and every stall in human growth and development can be placed at the door of these rascals.

How can you tell real spirituality from rampant fundamentalism? I think there are three telltale signs:

1. *Fundamentalists are sure they are going to heaven.* I believe it is important to have a certain measure of "faith" about our salvation. You can have confidence without overbearing arrogance. After all, there is a reckoning coming.

2. *Fundamentalists know how to get you to heaven.* If God is a spirit, as He claims to be, I seriously doubt if He can be encapsulated into five sound bytes and three exercises in worship. Salvation is an individual journey, which should not be tainted by contrivance.

3. *Fundamentalists think you need to "give up" or "give in" to "get in."* If God looks on the heart, then God looks on the heart. Remember the warning

about cleaning the outside of the cup and leaving the inside filthy.

So, can you have religion without fundamentalism? Yes—for it is possible to have a home without having cockroaches. But it is not possible to live in an apartment or house next to someone who has them. It is not possible to keep the moist climate and food available in the house and not welcome the filthy varmints.

Any religious experience that focuses on the pursuit of godliness and enforcement of moral codes is the breeding ground for the infestation of fundamentalism.

Spiritual gold is not the pursuit of God. God is everywhere. He does not hide. Spiritual gold is the discovery of our personal responsibility extending into the brotherhood of mankind.

When I was twenty-six years old, I wrote a musical play called **Mountain**— an adaptation of the Sermon on the Mount set to music with dramatic and comedic sketches and choreography. It was 1978. I was excited. The piece was good—at least as good as I could do at that time in my life. A friend of mine helped raise money. We recorded the music, put together a cast, and booked a twenty-five-city tour across the United States—quite a feat.

I arrived in Atlanta, Georgia, at one of our first performances. Our cast was filled with college students—eager, energetic and spiritually enthralled with the subject matter and the sheer, wild abandon of the journey.

We performed that night. There was a state senator from the Georgia legislature present who was one of the sponsors of the event. Unfortunately, a half-dozen people had walked out when the play began because there was dancing, and they felt it inappropriate for a religious production.

After the show, I was called into a small office filled with doctors, lawyers, people from the local city council, teachers, ministers, and, of course, the state representative—all in all, about twenty people.

I was asked to sit down and then was informed that they had been greatly offended by the addition of dance to this production on Matthew 5 through 7.

"Does dance appear in the Bible?" I asked.

"Yes," was the answer, "but not choreography."

"So the Jews danced without choreographing it? Wouldn't that be

21

risking the danger of running into each other?"

They didn't like my smart answer. Religion just doesn't seem to like "smart" all that much. It's not that religion is stupid, just that being smart might lead to the spreading of new ideas long before the committee has granted approval.

They explained to me that dancing leads to lust.

"Lust? Well, so do church secretaries, organists and ministers, but I don't see anyone giving up letter-writing and hymn singing."

Once again there was a disapproving grunt from the participants because of my lack of soberness on the issue.

"Let me save you time," I said. "Neither one of us is going to convince the other of anything this evening. I understand that I'm fighting an uphill battle in a day and age when playing it safe is the only game in town. I had to cancel a date in Mississippi because they asked me if we had any black members in our cast. To my chagrin, we don't. But I canceled the date because they asked. Now you fine, intelligent people in this room would never allow yourselves to be acquainted with that form of bigotry,

22

because now, here in Georgia, that level of prejudice is passé. More suitable for Mississippi, right? But what you don't understand is, the level of bigotry you've expressed towards a cast of very excited young people tonight about dancing will be, in a very few short years, just as passé and make you look just as ignorant."

I left the room. I was fairly confident. Why? Because anything that brings joy to the hearts of people and unites them in a common good is full of the breath of God. And what God has joined together no man will be able to tear apart.

It was less than ten years later, while passing through Georgia, I noticed an advertisement from the church the state representative attended. It was a notice about praise dancing during worship services. I smiled.

Joy will make a way. Liberty will have its day. And God will not allow people to be bottled up by tradition forever.

If your religion is filled with shouldn't

Then truthfully dear souls, I wouldn't.

If it is speckled with an abundance of can't

Then really feel free to say, "I shan't."

23

If it favors one over another
Then leave it alone, my brother.
And, most definitely, if it chooses to hate,
Leave—before it is too late.

Sitting Four

There have been times in my life where I was certainly overly cautious and conservative, and other times where it seemed my liberality was off the scale. In both cases, somebody always got hurt. Usually, in my excessive liberal moments, it was a self-inflicted wound to my own consciousness or physicality. And in the case of my more conservative junctures, the injury inflicted was usually upon others by my over-zealous self-righteous posturing.

I have a memory of being in front of a classroom of my friends and decrying rock and roll—claiming it was devilish and out to incite young people to immorality and insurrection. I remember seeing the blank stares on the faces of my classmates, totally bewildered by my sudden inclination to reject a kind of music I had previously enjoyed.

I hadn't come to this position on my own.

When I was about fourteen years old, the men in our church decided to attend a religious retreat in the mountains of Oklahoma—five days in the wilderness with 3,000 men and no women except for the couple dozen who were ushered in to cook and serve. These elders in our church concluded it would be a good thing if some of the young men joined in on this trip. I was one of them

I don't remember much about the drive, but I do remember that the adults controlled the radio on the way, and I was thrilled when they allowed Gerry and the Pacemakers to sing *I'm Telling You Now* all the way through without flipping the channel.

We arrived in the Oklahoma wilderness and then drove deeper into the depths of the mountains and forest, I assume because just average wilderness was not retreated enough to find God. It was rattlesnake country, and every year before this gathering, they would put a bounty out on the rattlesnakes—a dollar a skin. This particular year, they had paid out well over a thousand dollars.

I wasn't sure whether that comforted me or not. It meant there were a thousand less rattlesnakes in the bush, but of course, who's to say they didn't bag the real slow dumb ones, and the smart ones were just waiting, salivating, if snakes do such a thing, for some young fat boy from Ohio?

The campground was rustic— certainly an understatement. Hard wooden benches with no backs. It was mid-May and already steaming hot. It was open-air, all outdoors, complete with bugs, humidity and the unforgettable smell of 3,000 men stewing in the heat.

The speakers were endless, not only in number, but also in duration and themes. Still, there seemed to be a common thread amongst it all—America had fallen from her lofty spiritual heights and needed to wake up, repent and come back to God's will.

There were authors, craftsmen and sales folk everywhere, peddling everything from Indian jewelry to postcards with pictures portraying Martin Luther King, Jr. at a meeting of the Communist party. (Actually, the photo was a picture of a large gathering with one tiny black head circled; we were just to understand that the circled head belonged to MLK.)

There was one dusty road that led to a tiny store—a friend and I made the trek with the hopes of picking up some candy bars but discovered their idea of such confections was limited to brown paper sacks of horehound candy. While we were in the store, a young boy, perhaps ten, came in—a Native American. He asked for a pound of bacon. The man behind the counter sliced him off a piece from a big slab. The young Indian gave him his money and walked out of the store and the clerk laughed.

"That little savage was so stupid he didn't even know I cut him off just fat." There were several good ole boys nearby that provided the laugh track. I laughed a little, too, but felt like crap about it. I bought a book there, called "Rhythms, Riots and Revolutions." It told me that rock and roll music was of the devil and found its roots in the African beats of tribes that were cannibals and part of the evolutionary realm of the monkey.

Looking back now, I feel very silly about having even read the tome. But I was a kid, trapped on a mountain in the middle of nowhere, at the mercy of men who should have been my leaders but instead were enslaving me to the very worst of ignorant rhetoric and bigoted tradition.

We slipped away one day into the woods, walking very quietly so as not to disturb any snakes that had survived the killing competition. Suddenly, there was the loud sound of crackling, broken branches, and this man dressed in buckskin emerged from the woods. We were a bit startled.

He looked at us and said, "What chew boys doin'?"

"We're looking for a place to swim."

He pointed us to a nearby creek but warned us it was mountain-fed and was going to be ice cold. He then said, "Why you bein' so quiet out here?"

I replied, in a half-whisper, "We didn't want to alarm the snakes and bring them to attention."

He laughed. "Well, you should walk as loud as you kin, 'cause you certainly don't want to sneak up on 'em, now, do you?"

This made complete sense. We noisily found the creek, took off all our clothes, and slid down the bank into the ice-cold water. All of our parts shrunk back in terror. We swam around until the water felt almost normal, although I'm sure I never felt my toes.

We finished up the week in the mountains, and I was very glad to get on the road. Although I was temporarily enamored by this patriotic, religious fervor, and even though it caused me to become overwrought for a season, I think, in a strange way, it vaccinated me from future infection. I think it showed me clearly how being overtly conservative tends to be a self-punishment we wish to inflict on others because it hurts so much inside ourselves.

It made me realize that if you're going to take impressionable young men somewhere, it should be on a journey to discover their own souls and to teach them to be more open to others. And finally, it made me understand that everything has been placed in life to help us find the balance—everything from rock and roll to all-male clinics in the mountains of Oklahoma.

Oh, and by the way, I wasn't just inflicted by irrational fundamentalism. When we slid down that bank, we slid right through some poison sumac. So, for the next six weeks, I had an ongoing reminder from the trip. It took a long time for me to put that . . .. behind me.

Sitting Five

If you want to find a banana, just follow the monkeys.

Seems reasonable enough. Of course, the only problem with that philosophy is, when you get there, there's an awful lot of monkeys vying for the same banana—not to mention the scary gorilla who just might show up.

I have never been a contented follower, and it's not so much because I don't enjoy allowing someone else to be in charge. Rather, it's more that I grow weary of being in the mass hysteria of "vying for the same banana" amongst all my fellows who are aping the status quo to gain acceptance. I guess I've always preferred attempting to become the banana and letting the monkeys find me.

When I was eighteen years old, one afternoon, I slipped into the back of my mother's loan company and sat down at an upright piano that was kept there for reasons that now escape me. I began to write songs—two that first day.

I called a couple of friends and played the songs for them. They were very respectful of my efforts but also very negative about the potential of ever getting anything recorded or published.

Honestly, they just wanted me to settle down and get a job and be normal. I can't fault them for that—they were just preaching what they lived. They were monkeys heading for the banana (and I mean that in the most respectful way possible.) They didn't believe that we mere mortals had either the capacity or the purpose to construct our own banana.

In all candor, I was temporarily overcome by this philosophy. I went out looking for work. My God, it's a jungle out there! I got a job delivering medical specimens but got fired because I didn't have enough money to buy dry ice and delivered some blood tests at room temperature—a real no-no, I found out. I tried to sell Grolier encyclopedias door-to-door but one day, while calling on a gentleman at his home, I misunderstood and stepped inside, thinking I had been invited. After I left, he called the police and said I had forced entrance. I spent a half hour at the police station explaining my mistake. The job only lasted two days for me—my personal reenactment of "Death of a Salesman."

I played Santa Claus in a department store and did so well that they asked me to stay on after Christmas and work in the store. In my youthful glee, I was anticipating a management position and ended up as a stock boy. One day, when they sent me out to corral the shopping cart, I just walked off the job, got in my car and left.

I tried to be a loan collector for my mother's business but found myself too sympathetic to people's excuses and plights.

Then one day, I got a job delivering dry cleaning bonds—coupons sold over the phone for discounts on dry cleaning to willing patrons. It was the dead of winter in Ohio. I had a 1958 Chevy, which blew air but had forgotten years earlier how to warm it on the way out. I had a pair of boots with a hole in the sole. I tried to keep the snow from coming in by inserting pieces of cardboard. (You don't have to point out that cardboard is not water-resistant.) I came home every night with frozen feet, tingling hands, thawing out just in time to get up the next morning and start all over again. It wasn't horrible—just made me feel like a monkey. A very cold monkey. I was quickly losing sight of the golden banana.

One day, I went to a door on the campus of Ohio State University. A young woman answered, and I explained I was there to deliver her dry cleaning bond she had requested over the phone. Well, as often would happen, she didn't understand that she was purchasing the bond—something the phone solicitors often failed to communicate. So I began to sell her, face-to-face, explaining to her how she would get twenty dollars worth of dry cleaning for only $7.70. About halfway through my spiel, I noticed her eyes glazing over. I was boring her. Or maybe I was bored, transfusing boredom into this hapless human. When I finished my speech, she looked up at me and dead-panned, "O.K., I'll buy it. But, why all the fuss over dry cleaning?"

I don't know what it was—maybe it was her question, her response, my fatigue, my nippy toes, or just my time to stop chasing the banana. But I thought to myself, "No crap. Why all the fuss over dry cleaning?"

I went back to the office and resigned. I got in my car and sang all the way home. Later that evening, I penned the words to my next song. I felt good. Everyone else was gravely disappointed.

Since then, I've had rich days, and I've had poor days. I've had days of plenty, and I've had days where the presence of nothing seemed to be my daily bread. I've had applause, and I've had jeers. I've been alone, and I've been surrounded by appreciative fans.

I've been scrutinized and lionized. I've been embraced, and I've been cast away.

But I've never regretted creating my own banana. It has its own appeal.

(Sorry.)

Sitting Six

I went through my twenties in the seventies. I was there for the Jesus movement, Watergate, Nixon's resignation, disco, pet rocks and plaid pants being cool (oh, wait, is that back again?). I was there at the inception of contemporary Christian music and had the privilege of working with Andre Crouch and performing in auditoriums, churches, coffee houses, street corners, schools, living rooms and, once, in the back end of a bus. It was a time when itinerant musicians were plentiful and people opened their homes to welcome strangers from the street for a night of hospitality, food and fellowship. I'm sure it still happens but certainly not with the same frequency and grace.

I was in Maryland. I was supposed to appear in a church on Sunday, but arrived two days early, so a kind lady from the congregation offered her home to our group. She wasn't going to be there, so she left the key and stocked the refrigerator. It was a little piece of heaven to us vagabonds.

We settled in, watched some television, munched until we could munch no more, and then headed for bed.

I couldn't sleep. Well, not exactly. It was one of those "I couldn't sleep" until the next thing I know, "I'm dreaming, so I must be asleep" situations.

I thought I heard someone call my name. The first time, I ignored it, slept on. Then it came again, a little louder, so I awoke with a start, my heart pittering. I wasn't sure I had heard my name called, so I lay there quietly for a moment to see if there was actually a voice. Nothing. I began dozing, sliding back into sleep, when there it was again. A female voice—yes, definitely a woman.

Well, I did travel with two girls, so it didn't seem very peculiar to me that someone might be calling, so I slid out of the bed and walked through the house to see if one of the ladies was trying to get my attention. But both of my traveling partners were sound asleep.

The house, which had seemed so inviting hours before, now seemed very still—foreboding.

I felt really silly to be spooked by the whole situation, so I went back to the bed and got under the covers. But I left the light on. (Okay, I was a bit unnerved.)

Just as I went back to sleep, the haunting call occurred again. Yes, it was a bit haunting; echoey. Even though all the voice said was my name, there was a pleading in the tone, almost plaintive, lonely. I was now officially awake.

Of course, my first instinct was to get everybody up and see who was playing the joke on me. Still, it didn't feel that way—like a joke, I mean. I turned on more lights. Somewhere in my cognitive memory banks, I had retained a recollection that disembodied voices were startled by light bulbs.

I walked through the house— perhaps I should change that to "prowled." Actually, I felt silly.

It was a fairly large house, and I really hadn't made the full tour when I first arrived, so in the process of my journey, I happened upon a room. Just a couch and a few chairs—I think there was a lamp—some scattered magazines, and on the wall was one picture. It was one of those photographs that had been artistically touched up to look like a painting; a young woman in her twenties, long brown hair, pug nose, blue eyes, and apparently somewhere, a voice.

It was her.

Yes, I really believed she was the one who had called my name. Before you throw the book across the room, assuming I'm a little tetched, understand that all strange things happen in the moment, and make sense for that time, never to be retrieved or understood in the same way again.

She was a picture. But for that particular milli-second of thought, I believed she had called me to the room. I thought about waking up my companions but wisely rehearsed in my mind the potential scenario. "Yeah, I was in my bed, and the picture frame called me to the room, by name, and so I thought I'd wake you all up to see if we can figure out what this wall hanging wants . . ."

Right! I'd keep my feelings private for the time being. I stretched out on the couch nearby and stared at the picture. The eyes seemed warm and moist—a strange blending of compassion and pain prevalent in souls damaged.

I must have fallen asleep because the next thing I knew it was morning. I looked up. The picture looked just like a picture in the morning light. Any sensation of urgency or importance had passed away. I felt ridiculous and a bit creaky from sleeping on a small couch all night.

Then the dilemma.

Do I trust my night spirit or my morning thoughts? Do I pursue the instincts of my mystified mind or follow the logic of my daytime doldrums? There is the question. I really believe this to be the huge quandary for any of us. I just find that there are always voices, dreams and inspirations trying to speak to us— often in the stillness of the night. But by the time we slurp down our morning coffee and slide down a couple of pieces of bacon, it feels so dumb to us, we dismiss the intervention to pursue the common.

I did try to put it out of my mind. I couldn't. This struck at the heart of what I believe. It just seems useless to me to pursue the worship of a God we have no personal contact with in the present. Honestly, if God only speaks to me through the Bible, I'm screwed. The Bible doesn't always make sense to me, and there are just times that I need to be enlightened.

I resisted the temptation to share my visitation with my friends. It really wasn't even a temptation. I guess I was a little selfish about it—it was MY spooky thing. It was MY vision.

That evening the lady of the house returned. She was a delightful woman in her late forties, breezy and easy to talk to. We all chatted through the evening and, after the girls had gone to bed, I mustered up the courage to ask.

"Who's the girl in the picture?"

Her eyes immediately welled with tears. It was so sudden that I was a bit startled. "I'm sorry," I said. "I didn't mean to . . ."

I wasn't sure what I didn't mean to do. But for some reason, my question had created some instantaneous sadness in my hostess.

She shook her head. "No, no. It's not you. The girl in the picture is my daughter. She lives in Baltimore. She's on drugs, and she tried to commit suicide."

I sat for a long moment. I wanted to tell her about my dream, but I felt foolish. Or maybe I thought it would sound a little manipulative, like I was trying to make some sort of personal contact with her that was out of line. Fortunately, she continued.

"I haven't seen her for six months. I come in here, and I sit and pray for her. But I know the reality is, at any moment of any day I could get a call saying that she has overdosed or has killed herself."

She burst into tears. I wanted to hug her, but it was a little too intimate for the time span of our knowing each other. I reached over and patted her shoulder. She continued to weep, as she apparently had many times before.

So what was I going to do? I could console or I could confide. Consoling is so much easier. The hand reaching across the room to comfort is so much more palatable to the human ego than the decision of cracking open the heart and exposing the common pain. We just sat, then said goodnights and went to bed. But guess what? I couldn't sleep. I was ticked at myself. I realized I had passed over a gentle moment, an eternal juncture; a passage of time between two people that rarely happens; ordained from heavenly places and fostered by angelic notions.

Yes, I did it. I got up and went and knocked on her bedroom door. She spoke through the door. "May I help you?"

I felt so stupid. I was making her uncomfortable in her own home. "Yes," I said, clearing my throat. "I just would like to tell you something."

"Well, let me get my robe on," she said.

My God, this was too bizarre. She emerged from the room and stood in the hallway. And it was from that unnatural, clod-like position that I shared my story. I told her about the voice. I told her about the picture. I told her about sleeping on the couch. I told her about my doubts. I told her about—well, I probably ended up telling her too much.

She listened cautiously, like one would do when hearing such a story from basically a total stranger. She was respectful, honoring my sincerity. At the end of my discourse, she said, "Well, just pray for her."

"No," I replied. "I've spent my entire life just praying for stuff. It's like the great 'gesundheit' of life. When we don't know what else to say, we say 'we'll pray'."

I was befuddled. The golden rule does not begin with "pray." It begins with "do." I'm human. I've got to do something, or I'll go nuts. I continued. "Just trust me this far," I said to her. "We're performing at your church on Sunday, both in the morning and in the evening. Promise me you'll invite your daughter."

"She won't come."

"I know it seems that way."

"No, it is that way. I've invited her a thousand times to a thousand things with a thousand different approaches."

"Just one more."

"I'm not even sure how to get hold of her."

"Well, apparently you have a thousand times before."

Now I was annoying her. I decided to soften my approach. "Listen, you don't know me. For all you know, I could just be a little nutty. But what if I have had some sort of strange encounter with your daughter's spirit? I mean, is it impossible? I mean, if she was in real need and God wanted someone to know? Who could he tell?"

"He could tell me."

"Could he? After all the disappointment and sadness would you still have heard the cry with the same awe and wonder as some dorky stranger lying in your house? I don't know. It doesn't make any sense. Which makes me wonder. Do you understand? I mean, when I wonder, it is really the only time that stuff of God comes to my mind. When I just think, well, I just think about myself. But when I wonder . . . it's a time that God can crack my case and shed a little light on my dullness."

She smiled. She agreed to try to get in touch with her daughter. Then there was a simple series of tiny coincidences, which after, accumulated into a great heap of surprising occurrences greatly resembling a full-fledged miracle.

First, she actually believed me. Next, she called to try to find her daughter. Amazingly, she made contact. It was astounding that the daughter took the call and agreed to come to the Sunday night service. Still more outrageously fantastic, she arrived, sitting in the back of the auditorium in the most hostile profile she could portray. I didn't care. I sang, I shared, I opened my own heart, and I finished.

It all seemed so anemic, so riddled with human frailty. I was discouraged with my own inadequacy. This was a young girl that needed the voice of an angel or the roar of a prophet, and she was stuck with an overweight, traveling troubadour.

At the end of the service, I said, "I have had a most wonderful, intriguing and bewildering weekend. It would be too difficult for me to explain. But let me just say—well, let me just say something that will only make sense to one person in this room. It was 1:15 a.m. this past Saturday morning—that's right, yesterday—when I heard you call. I heard you call my name."

Then, there it was. I had never experienced the meltdown of a human soul quite like I did at that moment. This young girl who had sat through the entire presentation with the stoniness of a stalagmite, just dissolved in front of my eyes, every muscle relaxing, inhibitions melting away as she stood and walked to the front of the church and fell on my chest, crying.

We cried for a while. Then we talked. We did a little praying. She opened up her heart. She told me that, at that time Saturday night, she had made an ultimatum to the Almighty. "Prove yourself or leave me the hell alone and let me die." We embraced.

It seemed that He decided to prove himself. It seemed that she would never be the hell left alone. And I'm glad to report that she didn't die. I assume she went on to be a happy woman. At least as happy as any of us will allow ourselves to be. I never saw her or her mother ever again. I wasn't needed any more. I was fulfilled in knowing that sometimes, when things go bump in the night, they want to get our attention to do something— something wonderful outside of our little sleepy-time world.

Sitting Seven

Digging for gold. Of course, there is something called "fool's gold." Shiny rocks, not worth a lot—probably not anything.

When I was traveling with my musical group in the mid-seventies, we were invited to perform at a youth rally in Dayton, Ohio. I hated youth rallies. They were usually neither youthful nor did they rally much of anything.

In this particular youth rally, our group was given three assignments.

Number one: To provide the young folk an enjoyable, yet spiritual experience.

Number two: To "rock the house," which I knew from my experience, meant playing music ranging from Lawrence Welk to James Taylor.

And Number three: To close the event with an "altar experience"—something this mainline denomination could point to and say the youth rally was a success.

We began with a song. There was a smattering of obligatory applause. One of the youth directors stepped up and whispered in my ear, "I think the sound is a little too loud." I nodded dolefully, and we proceeded to the next song. An even lesser smattering of applause. Another youth director approached to again advise me on yet some other aspect of the sound.

The audience was so dead they would have had to climb a few rungs to achieve the level of boredom. We struggled on for some forty-five minutes—a process which can only be described as mutual torture. Finally, the time came for me to initiate assignment number three.

I cleared my throat and spoke to the crowd. "Is there anything anyone would like to . . . uh . . . share . . . with the group?"

An unexpected turn of events. A young man stepped out of the crowd and made his way to the front. He was so energetic and so assured I suspected him of conning me.

"What is it?" I asked.

"I would like to start over."

I gaped, astonished. Had God sent this remarkable young man in spite of my self-piteous tantrum? Still, I sniffed a con. I stepped toward him, but before I could reach him something happened. Something I had never seen before and will likely never see again. The young man appeared to pass out, and fell straight back, landing with his head in the lap of another young man. This second young man also fell backwards, his head landing in the lap of another fellow behind him, who repeated the process by falling into the lap of the person behind him. There were now four young men lying flat out on the floor.

Two adults stood up, approaching, presumably coming up to assist. But before they got very far, they, too, fell down in a seeming dead faint. Now some of the other youth began to stand up, probably planning to make their escapes, but before they could get to the door they were on the floor. I found my way to a chair to avoid being in the way of the falling bodies. The lead sponsor of the rally leaned over to me, whispering frantically, "What's going on?" I shook my head. Never in the history of the world has an "I don't know" been uttered with such complete sincerity. By the time the session was over, at least 90 of the 150 present were lying on the floor, many on top of each other.

Our music group was unaffected.

The next day it was the buzz of the church—morning, afternoon—actually, all week. A meeting was held to determine the cause and effect of the "fainting spells." It was decided that if our group were ever to be invited back, we should promise to control such hysteria and take steps to prevent all group passing out.

As it turned out, we were invited to come back the next year. We arrived, set up our equipment, performed our set, packed up and left. Not a swoon in sight.

God doesn't need to repeat himself. Furthermore, what we had experienced at that youth rally was an example of the *humor* of God. He just decided to do a miracle with an apathetic collage of young-uns. Miracles do happen, you see, but not because we pray them in or rock them out with our praise team.

I have since been in groups attempting to imitate and stimulate such events as the one I experienced with the youth rally. They generally leave me cold. They are fool's gold—shiny imitations of no real value.

What God gave us that day was real gold—an encounter with divine humor and power—and we didn't even have to dig for it.

Sitting Eight

I would like to take a few sittings of the book to discuss the elements of the human process. We are not a series of complex formulas, but rather, an existing work either in motion, stalled or digressing.

There are seven elements to the human process. If you understand these elements, you can pretty well pulse where you are at any given time, night or day, and then decide whether you want to move forward, stay where you are, or relax your effort.

First of all, life is not a marathon run; nor is it a sprint or even a walk. It more resembles a series of jogs followed by rest and reflection. The purpose of the jog is to attain something ahead of us that is important enough to pursue. The periods of rest and reflection are to prevent us from chasing our tails when we're not sure of our direction. It gives us time for recuperation, personal discovery and healing. With that in mind, what are the seven elements of the human process?

Number One: *Exist*
Number Two: *Observe*
Number Three: *Think*
Number Four: *Wonder*

Number Five: *Consider*
Number Six: *Feel*
    and
Number Seven: *Do*

These are the seven stations—stopping places and launching pads—for our human journey.

If you understand them you can use them to your advantage to get where you want to go. If you are unaware of their profiles, you could find yourself vegetating, unaware.

Let's start with Number One.

Sitting Nine

The first element of our human status is *exist*, which may I subtitle "sucking air without a prayer." There is much to be said for existence, for without it we would not be here. Yet, existence, in itself, is neither fulfilling nor motivating.

One afternoon, I was swimming in my pool when I happened to look up onto the pool deck and saw a bug lying on its back, legs flailing in the air. He had a problem (though it could have been a she, me not privy to the sexual parts of insect dudes).

He was incapacitated.

As I floated in the pool, looking at him, my eyes diverted for a moment, a few inches away, to where there was a carcass of another bug, also on its back, but this one quite dead and dried up by the sun.

So it was obvious what the fate of my little friend with the flailing legs was going to be if he couldn't get flipped.

Sometimes, I think about terms like "born again," "saved," "sanctified," "new leaf on life,"—and I realize how powerful they must have been when they were first spoken, in thought and in practice. Of course, over the years, their verbal pungency has been diluted by both misuse and overuse. Therefore I would like to introduce a new phrase.

GET FLIPPED.

I'm sure my little bug friend thought by flailing all of his little arms to the heavens he might improve his situation, although the carcass of a fellow-believer lay nearby—one who had pursued an identical approach. To continue to follow the philosophies, upbringings, concepts and doctrines proven to be ineffective is to suffer the fate of those hapless, trapped souls who lived before us.

My bug friend could wriggle, squirm, plead, struggle and jiggle his legs towards the sky all day long; he was going nowhere unless he took the time—or someone cared enough about him to help him—to "get flipped."

You don't have to be religious to believe your answers dwell in the heavens or in the sky above. Even scientists contend the only hope for Planet Earth is to escape into other galaxies.

While we are waiting for the heavenly intervention or the spaceships to leave, we might want to "get flipped," so we're back on our feet again.

My little friend was sucking air without a prayer. He merely existed. Getting flipped is acknowledging that if what we are is going to take us where we want to be, we certainly should have gotten some inkling from what is going on around us.

I reached over and gently nudged my little insect friend back onto his feet. He stood for a moment, wriggled his legs, shaking off the dampness, looked around and walked away. I thought I saw him pause for a moment and gaze at the corpse of his unfortunate predecessor. I wondered what he was thinking. I hope it was a mixture of sympathy and gratitude-sympathy for a friend who failed to get flipped and gratitude for the nudge that put him back on his feet.

Don't try to solve people's problems. Let them discover that they're just existing—"sucking air without a prayer" and then give them a nudge back to their feet. If they have even bug-sense, they will know what to do next.

Sitting Ten

The next step in the status of human development is "observe," which I have subtitled, "more than thee, begin to see."

During a rehearsal camp for a play I was directing, I put my cast through an effective emotional and mental exercise. We had the entire entourage of ten actors staying in the same facility. So I went through the living quarters, covering up all the mirrors with black paper. I then informed the cast that for the next twenty-four hours, they would not be able to look at themselves in the mirror.

"How will we know how we look?" one asked, puzzled.

"You will have to trust your other cast members to tell you when your hair needs to be combed or if you have a speck that needs to be removed from your face."

They giggled. Of course, their first instinct was to try to side step the experiment by attempting to catch a glimpse in the shiny toaster or a window's glare. I quickly retrieved my black paper and closed the door to such deception.

Then they became miffed and upset that I had suggested such an intrusion upon their person. How could anyone live without seeing oneself?

I explained that they would have to learn to trust others and learn to see the real appearance of nearby friends.

It took a while. But eventually, observation was set in motion. They began to help each other. They began to describe to one another specific grooming suggestions. It stimulated conversation. It opened the door to deeper understanding. For that twenty-four hour period, they learned to observe. It was "more than thee, begin to see."

It was a step away from existing— sucking air without a prayer—towards becoming a participant in the planet, an observer of the need, feelings and attributes of others.

They noticed things. They noticed subtle nuances in each other's appearances. They discovered what they really looked like through the eyes of others without having to stare at their own reflection.

Don't get me wrong—everybody was happy twenty-four hours later when I uncovered the mirrors. But for the rest of our camp and tour, we watched out a little bit more for each other. We began to observe "more than thee, begin to see."

Sitting Eleven

I've only used pain medication once in my life—I mean the heavy-duty stuff. You know, knock you in the head and drag you off to la-la land.

I had an operation and for forty-eight hours, they gave me a morphine drip, a little button so I could control my own dosage based upon my need to alleviate the pain. I was reluctant at first to use it, and only when I came back from a particularly grueling session of physical therapy did I finally push the magic plunger.

I don't remember much about it. I guess that's the whole point. It's not so much that morphine takes away your pain—it just removes you to a different corner of the room, where you kind of sit and eyeball your discomfort with abstract intrigue.

I remember during one of these particular stupors, some friends came to visit, wanting to carry on a conversation with me. I was really grateful for the company and wanted to contribute to the dialogue, but I noticed that every time I would speak, a puzzled look would come across their faces, and then they nervously looked at one another and changed the subject.

The morphine had taken away my ability to think. Unfortunately, I could still speak, but I made absolutely no sense (although one friend noted little difference).

I was so glad two days later when they rolled that infernal machine out of the room and I was able to retrieve thoughts again.

The third status of human development is *think*—"quite a find to use the mind."

Once you escape the rigors of mere existence (just sucking air without a prayer) you can begin to observe (more than thee begin to see.)

This stimulates the thinking process—"quite a find to use the mind."

Sometimes, I will turn to my teenage son and say, "What were you thinking?"

All he can produce is a dull stare and glassy eyes. He can't think. It has been days since he has observed anything, and he is barely existing.

Thinking is in the third position of the human process, submissive to our emerging from a mere cloud of existence and passing through the maneuver to observe. It sets in motion the higher gifts of humanity.

Sitting Twelve

Wonderful: to be full of *wonder*. Sometimes, people make it all the way to phase three in the elements and stop at just thinking. Mere thinking can turn any avid seeker into a cynical mocker, because reality is not what it's cracked up to be and often needs some assistance to create newness of life.

This is where we, as humans, have been given the great gift of *wonder*. There are no more powerful words in the universe than "I wonder what would happen . . ."

For Edison, it was, "I wonder what would happen if you could light up a room using incandescent filament?"

For Dr. Martin Luther King, it was, "I wonder what would happen if all races could be judged by the content of their character?"

For Henry Ford, it was, "I wonder what would happen if you put an engine in a buggy and priced it where everyone could afford one?"

For Jesus of Nazareth, it was, "I wonder what would happen if God could come into our human lives?"

Wonder—"reaching a junction and seeking function." All thinking must turn into wonder, or we believe life has congealed into what we see and reason to be.

Wonder is the step in the process of humanity when we move out of the animal kingdom and into the realms of God. We ask ourselves the question, "Why not?" Wonder takes us to a divine intersection where we want our lives to work and make sense and not just exist so we can observe and think about the facts provided.

Wonder is when the angels touch the mind with the notion of an interacting God.

Sitting Thirteen

She came up to my book table, a little tentative, uncertain of herself. "May I make a suggestion?" she asked.

I paused. I do like suggestions, but I haven't developed patience for oblique criticism. I responded cautiously, "Sure, go ahead."

"Did you ever consider," she began, "putting some of your books on CD? I mean, reading them aloud so people could hear your voice and enjoy them?" She was terrified and embarrassed. I guess that would either make her "embarrified" or "terrassed." (I am determined to eventually add a new word into the American lexicon.)

The word in her question that captured my fancy was "consider." "Consider" is taking "wonder" from the marketplace of thought to the private bedroom of life. It is no longer mentally elaborating on what could be done, but actually formulating a plan of what I, as an individual, can do.

Consider is moving from "function to personal unction." It is taking that most holy step from seeing the possibility to envisioning the first step on the journey to achievement.

Here's what can be done now.

Here is what I can do.

Here is what I have.

It is like Andrew, from that Bible story, bringing the five loaves and two fishes to Jesus to feed the five thousand people. Although he did not believe it was possible for anything to be done with it, he still provided it for consideration. At some point in our human journey, we must move from philosophy to practical application. And it must begin with ourselves.

Although "What needs to be done?" is a powerful inquiry, "What can I do?" is the only question that changes the world.

Sitting Fourteen

For a brief moment in the vast history of Christendom, a phenomenon named the PTL Club burst upon the horizon, impacted American society and then blew apart in an inglorious explosion of excess and greed.

I was there in 1976—the 200th birthday of our nation. The biggest attraction in the South at the time—certainly in Charlotte, North Carolina—was Heritage USA, Jim and Tammy Baker and the PTL Club. It was Walt Disney meets Amy Simple McPherson meets Woodstock meets Acapulco meets the Salvation Army meets Maybelline cosmetics.

Our little musical combo managed to get scheduled on the show because the Rambos had recorded one of my songs, and there was talk in the industry about us being an "up and coming new act." Obviously, we were thrilled.

The audience for the PTL Club for the time was estimated at six to fifteen million, depending on who was taking the survey. We arrived at the magnificent, if not overstated facilities, in our beat-up brown van, feeling most fortunate to have a pass through the gate because I am not so sure the security guard would have let us in otherwise. They sent us to our dressing rooms, where we put on our best duds.

One of the welcoming ladies came in, looked at our clothes and said, "Oh, I'm sorry. I'll come back in a few minutes after you've had a chance to change into your costumes for the show." We giggled.

"This is it," I said to her. "Anything we change into will be downhill from here."

I'm not sure, but I think she quelled a gag reflex.

I thought we looked great. The girls were in brown gaucho outfits with boots, and I had on black pants, a gold shirt and a red and gold plaid sports coat, which really looked good back in such a time when plaid was "bad."

She took us to the set. The show had seven different sets, and on the day we appeared, there were four musical guests. Each guest stayed on their own set, and when the Bakers had a mind to go to a song, the lights would go up and the singers would perform.

The show was about to begin when I turned to the producer, and I said, "You might want to tell Jim that we have a song that features sign language."

Well, little did I know that I said the magic words. The Baker's were extremely competitive with Jerry Falwell, and Falwell always had a lady doing sign language in the bottom corner of his screen. So we performed our song and at the end of the show, when there was only time for one more song, Jim opted to go to our group, I assume because of the sign language. It was a cool sensation. We got the extra song. We were pumped.

After the show, we were packing up, getting ready to go back to our beat-up van, when our fashion lady stopped by and handed us an envelope. I opened it. Inside was a check for $250. I just about died. We had agreed to do the show—in fact, were honored to do it—never thinking we'd get money. And $250 to us was a LOT of money.

She also invited us to stay and eat lunch with the cast and crew. We went into this huge dining room with lavish chandeliers and sat down at an ornate table. There must have been about sixty people in the room eating. They brought us plates of the most delicious lasagna I've ever eaten. Just about the time I finished my lasagna, out walked two stewards carrying silver platters with what must have been at least one hundred 12-ounce sirloin steaks. They began to plop them down on everybody's plate. I was overwhelmed. Where I came from, lasagna was a meal, not an appetizer. I shook my head in disbelief.

At that point, I knew two things. The folks at PTL wanted you to live high on the hog—or in this case, the cow—and number two, the people at PTL were trying way too hard to prove they were successful.

Here's the drift. I was young and thrilled to be there. They could have patted my head and given me a corn dog, and I would have been honored to be a part of the whole, delightful process. Someone made the mistake of thinking that first-class means first-rate. First class is a state of mind—a generosity of spirit and a willingness of heart. First rate is the current market value of the highest price in premium on the present going attraction. We should strive for first-class but be leery of first rate. I will always believe that Jim and Tammy Baker performed a very important function for a very brief season. They made spirituality fun, young, contemporary and accessible to the masses. But they didn't need to do it so lavishly.

I learned a lot that day. I went out and cleaned up my van a little bit, because

I could and still stay within the budget God had given me. We spiffed up our clothes, still within the dictates of our conscience and financial parameters. We became a little more generous to other people because we had seen and tasted the generosity of the Bakers—but all within the boundaries of our own blessing.

And we expanded ourselves in the most logical way—by spiritually opening the door to freshness and new ideas and letting creativity produce new vistas and potentials for our outreach.

When did money ever become a replacement for an idea? And when did opulence ever surpass simple hospitality and gratitude?

Sitting Fifteen

In 1980, while living in Mobile, Alabama, my son Joshua Paul was hit and run by a car. Somebody just took a car, hit him, drug him across the pavement, backed up, and took off—unknown—never heard from again, leaving in his wake a piece of his hell.

We were left with a son with severe brain damage, a shattered body, contorted features and an inability to communicate to us in any normal way. He spent two months in the hospital. He was in a coma until one day, they explained to me, he was no longer unconscious, just incapable of responding. The nurses whispered in the halls. Words like "retarded," "cerebral palsy," and, of course, "vegetable."

They finally let us take him home. We were like spoiled children given a broken toy and then told to "go and play."

You must understand, we believed ourselves to be people of faith.

But God is always a little hard to understand. Especially when he sends crap your way.

We were a family of four who now had three, plus one other who needed our constant care. It was like a sucker punch right in the middle of your heart; surprising, angering—damning—all at the same time.

Most of our friends wanted to find out who had done this terrible deed. They wanted revenge. I didn't care about that. To hell with him. I wanted to feel the good things again. I needed some control in my life. We hadn't birthed our second child to have him physically and mentally crippled. Sometimes it's just hard to pray when you're really angry with the person you're praying to. I didn't blame God, exactly; I wasn't infuriated with Him. I just had no idea what He expected us to do with this mess He had left for us to maintain. We were ill-suited to be the caretakers of a debilitated human being. I was way too selfish.

I worked on getting my heart pure, but when it was all said and done, what frustrated me was that I just couldn't go back and have things my own way. A new way had been deposited to me—not one of my desire nor of my making. I was not willing . . .

So then the thought came. It was gradual at first but then came more easily—made sense. Of course. We needed a miracle. Yes, I wanted a miracle, and for a thousand reasons— most of them noble.

Joshua had been home for just one day when I drove to the grocery store and bought four pounds of pork chops, two boxes of Shake 'n Bake, two bags of French fries, two large containers of peas and carrots and a strawberry cream pie. I brought the food home, sat Dollie and Jon Russell down and declared, "We're going to fast for three days. On the morning of the third day, we're going to put our pork chops on to bake, fix our meal and go into the living room and call Joshua Paul by name."

You see, this was my plan: the foods I had purchased were all of Joshua's favorites. It was my intention to call his name and have him walk out of his bedroom totally and completely healed and then the four of us would sit down and eat his favorite meal, rejoicing.

God, I felt in control again. We were going to solve our own problem with God's great cooperation. What was I saying? With God's *approval*. Isn't healing His will?

For three days, we fasted, each one of us feeling more empowered by the moment and intoxicated by the notion of our own faith and our own authority growing over this bizarre injustice. Only once did young Jon Russell question the validity of our project. We gently, but firmly, rebuked him for his lack of faith and compassion for his brother. He cried. We felt a twinge of mean-spiritedness, but after all, disbelief had to be challenged— or the miracle might just run away.

Of course, I was filled with doubts, too, but I drowned them in a sea of prayers and a deluge of scriptural promises, all tinged with illusions of the miraculous. It just made sense. Joshua needed to be restored. Whole was better than half, right?

The third morning arrived. Dinner was prepared. The three of us retired to the living room to begin our vigil. It all seemed so scriptural, so godly, so much like the Bible. Didn't Jesus rise on the third day from the dead? Wasn't three a holy number? Wasn't fasting something good people did to get God's attention? Wouldn't Joshua's miracle bring great glory to God? Conversions to the Christian cause? Where was the downside?

It seemed so heavenly.

We sat and prayed. And then, in unison, we called across the house. "Joshua. Joshua!"

Stillness—quiet—our voices echoed in the walls. We listened for the faintest stirring.

Nothing.

Of course, this was to be understood. Our faith was being tested. We called again. "Joshua! Come here!"

We varied our pleas, offered enticements. We told him about the pork chops. We mentioned the strawberry cream pie. The house was relentlessly silent; not a sound from the street, no telephone ringing. It seemed like the whole earth stood breathless to witness this endeavor.

We continued our calling for about half an hour. Nothing emerged from Joshua's room. Not a sound was uttered other than our pleas. We prayed more. But how much prayer does it take to conjure a miracle? Perhaps we should "tarry," whatever that means? Preachers, evangelists and the sort are never quite clear on that.

Did we feel foolish? Of course. But isn't foolishness part of the process? "Fools for Christ's sake." Isn't that what the Bible says?

After about an hour, any passion I had for the project had dissipated to a headachy weariness. Still, I didn't want to give up the dream.

"We have made a start of it," I said to my little family. We all smiled and agreed. For the pork chops were smelling really good, and we were only human. We went in and each of us gave Joshua a hug.

We told ourselves he looked better.

We set him up at the dinner table the best we could, and then we ate pork chops, French fries, peas and carrots and strawberry cream pie and . . . *pretended* . . that everything was all right and our mission had not been folly.

It was many months, maybe years, before we gained any understanding. We had failed to recognize that third morning what the real miracle was. The real miracle was that we were all together and the times and purposes were being unfolded to us in the daily rate that we as people could handle. And that God had silenced the earth so that not even a buzzing fly could make fun of our tempestuous turmoil.

I remembered some words. "Man was not created for the Sabbath. The Sabbath was created for man." It took time to understand this. For so long, I believed my ongoing, never ending responsibility was to find new ways to please God. What a joke! Mr. Universe is certainly more brilliant than that. God can't wait for us to "ascend" to heavenly levels of practice and understanding. He wades into the earthly goop and meets us in the midst of the melee and joins US in the mess.

Now I understand that my entire spiritual journey is learning to appreciate that God is already pleased with me and wants me to discover how comforting that can be.

May it wash over my soul.

Sitting Sixteen

Sitting in my office one day in Shreveport, Louisiana . . . wait a second. Way too pretentious. It was hardly an office. Just an itsy-bitsy side room in an H & R Block building I had rented for a tiny community outreach we had begun.

We originally called it "Artists Haven"—a spiritual sanctuary for creative people who wanted an outlet for their talents and fellowship with other scrawlers. Eventually, we changed the name to "The Haven." It was just a handful of people who got together, wrote plays and music, produced a few television programs and generally tried to impact our world in the most gently disruptive way possible. Although a mere couple dozen, our youthfulness and passion made many people in the community think that our numbers were much larger.

Meanwhile, back in that little room, the phone rang. It was a friend of mine, an older lady who told me she wanted me to talk to a man who recently had arrived into town and needed some advice. His name was Ned, and he was going through a rather rough time and desired some counsel. Although I was never comfortable with the idea of being a counselor, I certainly could provide a set of ears and maybe a little experience to some situations.

She closed her conversation by telling me that Ned was an evangelist in a tent revival. I had never been to a tent meeting. My image of tent revivals was limited to TV and movies and conjured up images of charlatans, snakes and fainting ladies. Still, no reason to hold that against old Ned, so I agreed to meet with him.

Ned came to my office. He had a large, red pompadour hair-do, fancy jewelry dangling from various areas of his body, wore an expensive jogging suit and enough self-assurance to bolster a whole room of teenage geeks. But still, Ned had a problem.

Ned liked women.

Now, there's nothing wrong with liking women.

But Ned didn't like women that way. Ned liked women best when they were lying down. I suppose someone with qualifications and more study in the matter might say that Ned had a sex addiction. Ned didn't see it that way. He looked on it as more of a secondary thrust to his mission. First and foremost was his

78

calling to preach the glory of our Lord and Savior, Jesus Christ. But, in the process of doing that, if some fair maiden needed more extensive laying on of hands, he felt inclined and anointed to accommodate.

Of course, I had known for years that most religious principles terminate slightly south of the belly button. Truth is, God has most of us from the lungs up. The heart and the stomach are battlegrounds, and what dwells beneath is a no-man's land—trench warfare.

Ned wanted to talk to me because his wife was becoming upset with his faithless philandering with the more fleecy of the flock. Ned, like most of us, had developed his own philosophy concerning such things. He felt as long as he was traveling with his tent crusade and not unloosening his Bible belt more than twice in each town with consenting young God-gals, well, basically, there was no harm.

How he came up with that equation I will never know. But it made perfect sense to him. Then he shared about an additional problem. He had fallen for one of the young women in our town (who he later confessed to me, was a third conquest within the same village limits, concluding that was probably why God had punished him, because, for some inexplicable reason, he had become attached to this one).

He said what saddened him the most was that she wasn't a very experienced woman and that he felt he had taken advantage of her. Of course, my mind was thinking of a fourteen-year-old nun, so I asked, "What do you mean by not very experienced?"

"Well," he said, "She hasn't had more than twenty men."

I paused. I quickly had a flashback into my paltry sexual history and yearned to say, "Goll-ee." But at the same time, not wanting to come across as inexperienced myself, or as some sort of prude, I refrained. "Twenty, eh?" I mustered.

He nodded dismally. He continued his story. On and on, we talked. Ned had a lot of nervous energy. He couldn't sit still without shaking his leg, like a tick hound with a twitch after a particular good scratching. He invited me to the "crusade." I agreed to come to the tent to see Ned preach. I spent the afternoon trying to envision what the evening would hold. It took me a while to figure where to sit so as to make a hasty exit if snakes were to appear or if, God forbid, the really experienced women were to approach me.

Tent revival: loud, brash, arrogant, overly simplistic, demanding, flagrant, provincial, poor, dimly lit. Uncomfortable chairs. And hot. All the things one would normally associate with an evening out at the theater.

But still, Ned was sincere. He really wanted all of us to be delivered of our demons. He really wanted us to come forward so he could get his hands all over us and God could "grab a hold of us."

Don't get me wrong—there were some really sweet moments. At times, the experience was endearing. Perhaps it even would have had a community feel to it had it not reeked of backwoods fundamentalism.

Allow me a moment to digress. Religion feels the need to have an "enforcer," and fundamentalism is the mafia of religion. It gives us all an "offer we can't refuse." It keeps us beholden to the faith, reminding us of every payment we have due to the cause. It constrains us by its strength and intimidates us with fearful tactics and warnings of pending doom if we don't follow the party line.

It makes victorious people self-conscious.

It makes self-conscious people dependent.

It makes dependent people suspicious.

It makes suspicious people critical.

It makes critical people vindictive.

It makes vindictive people dangerous.

It makes dangerous people determined.

It makes determined people miserable.

And it makes miserable people evangelistic.

After the removal of communism from our planet, fundamentalism, either religious or secular—a belief in a singular, divine way for living—became the sole cancer eating away at the potential of the thriving living organism of humanity.

Here is how this monster of fundamentalism affected Ned. He was a good man with a problem. Fundamentalism turned him into a self-righteous man with an excuse.

Ned and I struck up a friendship. He was generous, talkative and fun, as long as you kept him off the subject of religion. When he went into his evangelist mode, he was pious, hypocritical, judgmental, narrow-minded and ranting with religious rhetoric. When he was human, he recognized his lusting for women as a weakness. When he was "tent guy," he had no weakness—just a thorn in his flesh that the devil tried to use against him.

When he was just Ned, he could talk about his wife and her complaints and what he might be able to do to change his direction. When he was the fundamentalist, his wife became Jezebel and all the women of the world were out to tempt him to get him to fall from his ministry.

He was two men trying to live in the flimsy skin of one. I liked Ned. The revival dude you could have, but I liked Ned.

One day, I explained to him that God liked Ned better than Reverend Ned. He was offended. I didn't see him much after that. I regretted my candor—perhaps I should have been more diplomatic.

But, sooner or later, we all must speak out against the fundamentalism creating the strife and wars in our world. It's necessary that we do this—for ourselves, for our children and for all the Neds in the world.

Sitting Seventeen

I have done many crazy and wacky things in my life but perhaps none as bizarre and out-of-the-pocket as the mission I launched with my family in 1984 through 1988.

Having completed my work in Shreveport, I checked my children out of school, and we climbed into a van and took off to see America. The oldest boy was learning bass guitar, and my eight-year-old had become extraordinarily attached to the drums.

Our plan was really quite simple: we would arrive in a town on Monday morning, take out a weekly rate at a motel or available apartment facility, and my wife, Dollie, would get on the phone and inform the area pastors that the Cring family was in town and available—for this week only! —to come and share at their church.

Spontaneous became synonymous with the Cring family.

We had no extra funding whatsoever. We solely lived off the offerings and book and tape sales from our excursions.

We had no home address and didn't even have a credit card.

Needless to say, not all the churches and pastors were enthralled with our traveling concept. Some were negative—almost insulted—that we believed we could waltz into their town on such short notice and actually find an open door to ministry.

I have to be careful when I look back on it now, because what really seemed like such a good idea at the time is a source of embarrassment to me in the present.

But then again, shame on me.

I really believed God wanted me to do it. It is impossible, in a later season, to second-guess an action of faith in the now.

We traveled from sea to shining sea—saw cities all over this great land. We met some of the finest people in America and endured some lesser fellows.

By day, Dollie would call, and my kids would read, play, watch television and spend time with their old man. I developed a bond with my sons that could never be broken. We were fellow-laborers with a common need and a most uncommon cause.

Because our scheduling and approach was not prefabricated but rather launched in the moment, we were able to cross ethnic and racial lines as will.

Often, we would arrive at a black church, and they would be shocked that we were white, but by the end of the evening, each of us would become colorless.

Sometimes our mission took us into the inner cities of America, and other times we languished in suburbia.

We never quite knew what was next, and we learned not to question the beauty of being led and finding provision from the least likely sources.

It is not something that I would ever recommend that anyone else do, and I'm not even sure that it would be possible in our present-day climate, but for a moment in time, we lived on the land, through the land and for the land. For a time, we were angels unaware, touring the country, trying to spread a little good cheer and a ton of practicality. It was thrilling, dangerous, exciting, reckless, radical and righteous all at the same breath.

I have a thousand stories, too numerous to place within the confines of this small book. There were so many nights when we went into a performance with a financial need in front of so few people, barely enough for a dinner party, and we walked out the beneficiaries of a full-fledged monetary miracle and a human blessing.

We prayed for people, and they prayed for us. We laughed. We cried.

My sons missed opportunities to be on sports teams but gained experience in the real competitions of life. We stayed in one place long enough for them to make friends and even to date some young ladies.

I almost didn't share this chapter of my life in this book, because it's difficult to get someone else to understand what you don't totally even understand yourself. But I felt it was important for you to know that the only real criterion for inspiration is confirming that you hear the voice coming from within, because it rarely jives with the noise and confusion bombarding from without.

If you learn to trust the inner voice, it will take you down paths simultaneously fulfilling and lonely; solitary and enriching. Can you be wrong? Can you hear your own voice? Sure, but it becomes obvious very quickly. This you can be sure of: truth is always the minority opinion trying to find a voice, and tradition is always the majority opinion on its last legs.

So I say thank you to my family and the countless people we met over the years on our journey. It is my prayer that we were of benefit to you as much as you were of benefit to us, and it is my sincere hope that God will call others to be just as charged by a dream for their time as we were in ours.

Sitting Eighteen

I weighed twelve and a half pounds when I was born. They said the day after my coming out, I was already lifting my head up and looking around. I don't remember ever being anything but plump. I never wore regular jeans—always huskies.

My baby fat got a transfer and became teenage fat, gladly taking the downtown leg to Adultville.

I had three saving graces in the whole process. I was a pretty good athlete, playing a little football and a little basketball. I was funny—and not just looking. And I had a great love, if not talent, for music.

But I was fat. I never went in for craze diets, always staying pretty healthy with a good intake of fruits and vegetables, but I was fat. Oh, I already said that.

I guess I just want you to hear me say it. It's not that I'm proud of it—I really don't think there's anyone who is happy being fat.

But I have learned to work with it. I have benefited from the experience—not so much physically, as emotionally and spiritually.

I always had a great fondness for the ladies, and I really do believe I would have done a lot more stupid things and hurt a lot of good people if I had been even reasonably handsome in appearance.

Being fat forced me to focus on my inner man, my personal feelings, and discover my voice—what I really wanted to say—to the people around me.

I don't know what it's like to be neutral—to portray no particular vision to people looking on. I've always been fat, so I knew immediately upon meeting people that they knew I was fat as well.

But it did give me the advantage of knowing if someone took me seriously, or was impacted by my message, or relished some aspect of my personality or talent, it was totally legitimate, and not a byproduct of my appearance.

I'm not trying to say that being fat was, or is, a good thing or trying to rationalize my inadequacies. I just believe that, while we're waiting for the next thing to happen, it really doesn't hurt us to work with what we've got.

I don't know if I would have stayed married for all these years if I had been more immediately appealing to the opposite sex.

I don't know if I would have remained the father of my children if other options had been readily available.

I don't know if I would have misused the power of my position and the gift of my anointing, such as it is, if I had been able to rely on physical appearance in any way, shape or form.

I have a wonderful blessing in my life—I know that when people are moved or ministered to by my gift, it is because the spirit has drawn them, not because I've seduced or beguiled them by my charm or good looks.

Is there a sadness that accompanies that? Do I wish that I were more physically appealing? Do I desire a more acceptable countenance? I really don't know, because I really don't think about it.

I just figure if you work on the gift, people will just naturally not be so picky about the giver. If you accentuate the contents, the packaging will lose a measure of importance.

I don't like being fat.

Do I do anything about it? Yes. A thousand things in milliseconds every day. But so far nothing that has added up to my birthing a new physical persona. Is that in the cards for me? I guess we'll just have to wait and see if it's in my daily bread—or perhaps better stated—my lack of daily bread.

Sitting Nineteen

He had developed a cough. I didn't think much about it—he was twelve years old and even though he was incapacitated by the hit and run accident, he still was just a kid, and kids get colds. And anyway, Joshua didn't have a bad cough—just a little catch in the throat.

We were traveling across the country as a family. It was a unique arrangement. We had an old green van with a bed platform in the rear, where we laid Joshua on a mattress while we drove down the road. There were five of us—Jon Russell, fifteen at the time, Joshua, nearly thirteen, and Jerrod Micah, who was almost ten years old. We were traveling in the Pacific Northwest, near Eugene, Oregon. Joshua had been with us for six years since the accident, which had left him in a non-communicating, physically debilitated state, demanding constant care and needing to be fed baby food three times daily.

There was a problem. Although on medication, Joshua battled seizures. Sometimes, it was virtually impossible to get past his clenched teeth to give him the nourishment to sustain his frail frame. Let me say, no one ever feels prepared to care for a disabled child. The particular blending of moments of joy followed by flashes of guilt enhanced by perpetual fatigue drains the soul, exhausts the heart and leaves the body depleted of energy. It is truly a case of someone you love appearing to be the death of you.

There was a great bastion of hope that sustained us. A hope that a certain eye-blink meant he understood, or a facial expression connoted improvement or just lying down next to him and feeling his warmth for a brief interlude—these were the cherishables that made it all seem worthwhile.

His brothers took turns carrying him into churches, motel rooms, restaurants—many folks gracious and empathetic, some repulsed. It didn't make any difference. He was our son—a son who had now developed a little cough.

One night, while Dollie was feeding him, he coughed and blood came up. She sent one of the boys over with a towel speckled with blood, telling me to hurry to her side. We didn't know what to do. We didn't have health insurance. We were traveling around the country.

We knew that the presence of blood meant there was something wrong. It was also on the eve of my son Jerrod's tenth birthday. I had promised him that he and I would take out a separate motel room, so that we could have Dad and boy time and watch TV and order in a pizza together.

Now . . . Joshua was sick; blood ya' know.

I made a plan. Dollie took Russ and Joshua and headed for the hospital. I stayed behind with Jerrod, continuing our personal plans. About a half an hour later, there was a call. It was Dollie. The news was bad. Joshua had severe viral pneumonia.

Dollie came back home to spend a few minutes with Jerrod, and I went to the hospital. The doctor took me to the side and asked me what we wanted to do. I smiled—a smile of bewilderment. How could I possibly know what to do?

He explained to me that Joshua had been a miracle, both of God and technology. It was miraculous that he had survived this long. He stated that we could aggressively treat the pneumonia and put him on life support to sustain him—but we would probably be continuing a life that God was calling home.

I felt so inadequate to make such a decision. This was my son's life. Of course, I wanted him to live. Of course, I wanted the hope that he might get better. Of course, I was tired. Of course, I was bedraggled.

A collision of emotions made me feel unworthy to conclude the fate of another human being, especially when that human being was my son. I think the doctor understood my dilemma. He said, "Let's do this. Let's give him some antibiotics and be aggressive in our chemical treatment of him, but if his body does not have the strength to fight off this infection, let us both agree that his young body has warred long enough and should be given a chance to rest."

I nodded. I didn't understand everything he was saying, but it felt good to not have to move on anything right now.

Joshua lived through the night.

At ten o'clock the next morning, we faced another dilemma. We were scheduled to have a birthday party—a tenth birthday party—for Jerrod at a local kid's restaurant in town. Presents had been purchased and promises made.

I knew Jerrod would have understood if we had canceled the party, but I didn't want him to have to understand. I wanted him to have a tenth birthday party. So a friend of ours named

Steve agreed to come to the hospital and continue the vigil over Joshua, while Dollie, Russ, Jerrod and I went to a birthday party. Part of me wanted to feel guilty, but most of me knew it was right to go celebrate with a living son and leave my other son in God's hands.

We returned from the party, and the phone rang at the motel. It was Steve. He told us to get to the hospital quickly.

We hurried.

We didn't make it.

Joshua passed away about one minute before we walked back into the room. Sadness, frustration and guilt somersaulted inside of me, leaving me too weak to stand, nauseous and nearly breathless.

Steve told us he had gone quietly. I asked everyone to leave, and Dollie and I rested on the bed and held our son—our dead son.

It was six months before the dreams stopped. Nightly, I would dream about Josh, feeling a great urge to help him, save him, and bring him back to fullness. In my dreams, he was always alive.

In my memories, he has secured a place—a home in my thoughts—where I can never allow self-pity to find rest in me because recollections of his determination scatter them in shame.

I can never feel overly confident or arrogant about my status and wisdom, because I know how fragile and frail each of us can be. And I will never take for granted one single moment—one precious passage of tenderness, because I know the next breath, the next birthday, the next cough . . . could be our last.

Sitting Twenty

Back to those elements in the human process: exist, observe, think, wonder and consider. Quite a list so far. Are you moving freely amongst these five steps, or do you find yourself stuck in the "muddle?"

Two remain.

Jesus was moved with compassion. It says He was. Compassion is an oil to lubricate the engine.

The problem with ideas is that they find it difficult to make the journey from the mind to the heart. Let's be honest: we all need a little grease to slide our ideas into action. We need to FEEL.

I don't think we do anything merely by wondering what needs to be done and considering what we could do. It's the old parable of the "road to hell is paved with good intentions." As a matter of fact, the road to heaven is filled with signposts advertising great consideration.

What we need is a *feeling* to inspire us and propel us to action. What we need is a place to transcend thought and jettison some sort of seed—make a start of it. *Feel* is a sensation. *Feel* is "sensing the need and planting the seed." It is the flag flying in the wind, telling the world of our intention for liberty. It is the simple unearthing to grow a great notion. It is the bumper sticker on your car. It is the slogan placed on your stationery. It is the personal greeting on your answering machine. It is the warmth of your handshake. It is the breakthrough to correspond with a soul once forgotten. It is the phone call to the distant relative. It is the smile in the presence of gloom. It is the flower sent to the soul in despair. It is the meal purchased for that traveler in need.

It is "sensing the need and planting a seed" without any assurance that anything will grow but knowing that nothing will grow without the presence of the kernel.

Sitting Twenty-One

I have a neighbor who took the time to cultivate a small area of his yard to make a garden. He nurtured the soil and planted the seeds, and the rain came, and the plants grew, and with God's help and nature's efforts, he made tomatoes. I thought it was really impressive.

I'm always grateful for people who have gardens. I make a practice of hanging around them to obtain free produce.

The next year came around. He sowed his seed, but he didn't nurture the soil, and not as many tomato plants grew. The third year came along, and he sowed the seeds, but didn't nurture the soil, and weeds grew up all around, to where you could barely identify tomato plants from thistles. By the fourth year, he just didn't sow the seeds anymore. He has the largest crop of underbrush and tall grass I have ever beheld.

Many times, we will get as far as planting the seed, but we grow weary in well-doing, and we forget that the human journey is about "doing." Whether we see results or not. Because the option to doing is *watching*. And watching has a dastardly by-product of feeling helpless and out of control. At least, when we do something, we can show up believing there might be a harvest.

Do—"a physical reaction to a spiritual passion." What *feel* grows inside our soul as a passion, and that passion will not be calmed by promises, bits of scripture or isolated moments of devotion and prayer.   Passion needs to *do* something—it wants a physical action.

People often complain and say, "Well, I tried, but nothing happened."

But even if nothing is going to happen, don't you need the sensation and soul satisfaction of doing? We need to do, even when what's done leaves much undone and even more yet to do.

"Do unto others" is not a declaration to make something happen. It is a determination to create a happening, knowing that this is the only way to make something. It is rapid-fire, righteous rhetoric, rejuvenated repetitiously.

It is not "doing it until it works," it is "doing it because that is our work," and the alternative is an oblivious slide back into mere existence—"sucking air without a prayer."

So how does it work?

I *exist* so I can *observe*.

The process of *observation* causes me to *think.*

And because I can *think,* I *wonder* what could be done.

Which causes me to *consider* what I personally can *do.*

The process of *considering* creates a passion in me—a *feeling*—of wanting to reach out and do something.

So I reach out, and I *do.* Not because I am certain of the outcome, but because I am certain that I was created to *do.*

Sitting Twenty-Two

Women.

I tell my sons that their lives will be defined by what they decide about women. When you're a youngster, you have playing buddies. As a teenager, you have teammates. But you will spend most of your life with women.

I think many men err by supposing women to be opposite of men. Women are not the opposite of men. Women are men who have been sobered by tragedy, sensitized by emotion and enlightened by human frailty.

We come from each other, men and women.

I've had so many wonderful encounters with women over the years. I have a wife of over three decades, I've traveled with over a dozen different ladies while in the music field, I've been blessed with a second partner in music and traveling, and I developed an adult relationship with my own mother.

What have I learned, and what do I know? I know that women don't want to be men, but they do feel a great sense of mission to help us find our true selves. God said it was not good for a man to be alone. The first human creation was flawed more by need than by passion, so when God made woman, he corrected the designer's flaw with the hopes that we would find each other, join together and become one flesh—the essence of complete humanity.

Who is that complete human? He (or she) is a needy creature who, through passion, has exchanged need for want and is unafraid to pursue the dreams that lie deep within the soul and is willing to feel all the bumps and bruises that happen along the way. That brings me to my story.

My mother was a complex woman. One moment, she would be cleaning out her cupboards to give a morsel or two of food to a hungry family. The next moment, she would be gossiping and backbiting with all the vitality and verve of a cobra poised to strike and sling its venom.

She often had the annoying mixture of bouncing between being overly industrious and overly dependent. She had the infuriating habit of deciding to clean house when Saturday morning cartoons were just at their peak. She would simultaneously allow me to load eleven friends into our 1962 Impala to go to basketball practice and then rant and rave at the same chums because they wanted to watch Chiller Theater on Friday night in our living room.

Chiller Theater was evil. Twilight Zone was dark. She was blessed with the ability to listen but cursed with the predisposition to never let anything go.

I knew when I was twelve years old that I would have to begin to develop an adult relationship with her, or she would try to keep me a child all of my life. As I passed my teens and entered my twenties, she was often my worst critic. She never fully understood why I pursued the life of a vagabond musician instead of the security of the eight-to-five world. Though she had many friends, in her later years, she began to drive them away, to the point that in her last months she only had a few stubborn pals and three rag-tag cats.

Diabetes took most of her eyesight, and senility settled in much too quickly, much too certainly and much too obviously. She was placed in a nursing home. I received the news while I was living nearly three thousand miles away. I knew I had to see her again.

I planned a pilgrimage across the country with the entire family. We scheduled stops along the way and arrived in Ohio in the latter part of September. I situated myself in her little town and settled in to spend some time with her. I came to see her daily at the nursing home. She was grateful and seemed to be mostly aware of my presence.

I surrounded her in the experience of being near her grandsons (now three with the birth of Jasson, who had been born almost three months to the day after Joshua passed away)

But finally, it was the beginning of October and time for us to get on the road again. At this time, we were staying nearly thirty miles away, and I woke up one Saturday morning ready to leave town. I had this instinct to go see my Mom again, but it was a sixty-mile round trip and honestly, I just didn't feel like it. However, I had learned to mistrust those inclinations towards convenience over caring. I climbed into the car with the two boys and went to see her. We picked her up and took her to the local mall and purchased her some curly fries at Wendy's—her favorite. We bought her some sugar-free candy to take with her and then climbed back into the car to take her back to the home.

Out of the clear blue sky, she began to sing her favorite hymn—"The Old Rugged Cross." She never sang melody—always an off-key alto—about a quarter of a pitch from center. I sang with her. As I recall, the boys even joined in on the words they knew. We didn't discuss it. We didn't comment. The entire fifteen-minute trip back was spent singing that old song. We arrived at the nursing home, and my oldest son walked her in.

She stopped and turned and waved, and smiled and told us to be careful. I told her I would see her in two weeks, when we returned. We went on the road for that fortnight, and when we returned I called the nursing home.

They told me she had passed away. My brothers had been unable to get in touch with us on the road to tell us about funeral arrangements.

I was incensed. But then I was struck with a question. "When did she die?" I asked simply.

"She died on Saturday, October twelfth," the worker shared.

I don't even remember if I said "thank you" before I hung up the phone. October twelfth was the Saturday I had reluctantly driven the sixty miles to see her; the Saturday we had shared curly fries—the Saturday we sang "The Old Rugged Cross" together. I had been the last one from the family to see her. The journey was complete. I had driven three thousand miles across the country, spent two weeks in motel rooms visiting her daily, had motivated my sorry self to come and visit her one last time—for the honor, privilege and glory of being there when she was taken to the other side.

That is the power of an adult relationship with your mother and father, because when you cease to be dependent upon them, they can be dependent on you, especially in those closing hours, when they most certainly will need you more than ever.

Sitting Twenty-Three

Several years ago, Janet Fay Scott came back into my life. I had met her many years earlier, in Shreveport, Louisiana, and although we had stayed in contact, she was the Tennessee homebody and I, the itinerant of the Interstate.

She was going through a divorce and decided to move to Nashville to be closer to friends and a support group during the time of transition. She had three sons.

She also had a master's degree in music from Northwestern University, twenty-five years of experience in playing with symphonic orchestras, but was heading off, I thought reluctantly, to become a paralegal.

It seemed to be a real waste of her talent, at least in my opinion, but she just didn't feel like playing the oboe was a realistic prospect for her future. She needed a job and money.

I had written music all my life, as well as a few booklets here and there. With her arrival in Nashville, it seemed logical to me that we might want to team up and create a partnership in art and craft. It was just that simple.

It seemed a bit boorish to me for her to pursue my musical styling and to relearn a new vista of sounds when I could go ahead and write in a medium that she was more accustomed to performing.

So on one sunny July afternoon, I sat down and wrote my first semi-classical musical composition. It was interesting, if a bit sophomoric. She was thrilled. I was astonished. The world—well, the world just kind of kept twirling the way it always twirls.

But it was a beginning.

She helped me edit my novel, *I'M . . . the legend of the son of man.* I had been working on it for more than a decade, and together we commenced a jag of writing, me, the author and composer; she, the editor and musical scorer.

We were in the midst of working on my second symphony, when one day, in the studio, one of those haphazard thoughts sprang up. You know the kind I mean—half whim and half crackpot.

"Why don't we start a symphony orchestra?"

Aside from the fact that neither one of us knew how to do such a thing, and the consideration that it would be extraordinarily expensive, there was always the problem that we lived and worked in the middle of Country Music, U.S.A. Enthusiasm for violin work in our town normally began and ended with the phrase "fiddling around."

Did this stop us?   No—we were sufficiently intoxicated on our own delusion by this point.

So we started some fund-raising. Amazingly enough, there were actually some people who thought it was a good idea.   In the midst of this, I continued to write, completing four symphonies called **To Everything A Season**, a salute to spring, summer, fall and winter.

Drunken on our initial reception from the public, we planned our first concert for November of that year.   We held auditions and were shocked when musicians showed up.   We hired some of them and launched the organization we dubbed "The Sumner County Symphony."

Some people were supportive, others snickered at the idea of such an organism in our county, but everyone was intrigued.   We made one decision early on: all the proceeds from ticket sales from any event would be donated to countywide charities, including schools and band programs.   Of course, we were told that this was nice but not necessary and certainly implausible. For you see, the money to pay for the orchestra would have to come solely from advertising in our program book.

We held our first concert on November thirtieth. The place was packed, mostly with curiosity seekers and, I believe, people who just figured they needed to be there for the first one, because a second one would be unlikely.

I am happy to say they were wrong. We don't always pack our concerts, but we do have respectable attendance and countywide support, which is ever growing. We have been able to give tens of thousands of dollars to organizations, businesses, ministries, schools and individuals with needs and outreach to the community.

The partnership? It just keeps rolling on. Now, to date, with eight books to our credit and thirteen symphonic works, I learned a very valuable lesson. You can't always control what happens, but you can take what happens and reestablish control.

Ah . . . do unto hassle, as you would have hassle be overcome by you.

Sitting Twenty-Four

A surprise wedding. The idea seemed a little bizarre but also intriguing in its own way. Of course, the key to pulling it off would be to possess a certainty that both parties involved wanted to get married in the first place.

My son, Jon Russell, seemed to possess this certainty concerning his fiancé, Tracy. So he suggested during a particularly delightful vacation to southern Florida, that it might be nice if they get married on the beach. He explained to me that it had always been her dream to have a sunrise wedding on the beach, the ocean pounding in the background, and a few close friends around to celebrate the occasion and commemorate the event.

We decided to do it.

So on one Friday morning, we all slid away to go to the beach—twelve of us in all—under the pretense that we were going to have some sort of morning inspirational time during the sunrise.

Tiki torches had been placed, a spot decided, and plans made for a reception at a local sidewalk café. Well, it came off beautifully. Vows were exchanged, music was played, and a brunch consumed.

Aside from being a very beautiful experience, I will always remember that day for another reason. Upon arriving back in my motel room, I discovered that the big toe on my left foot seemed reddened—a bit inflamed with some scaly white skin on it. Honestly, I didn't give it much thought. Little inflammations like that were not unusual in traveling. So I doctored it a little bit and continued on my way.

The next week it got a little worse, and I became a little more intense in my care. Over the next month, it became more inflamed and infected—although in such tiny increments that I was never quite able to believe that it was something serious. I continued to hop airplanes and fly off and perform on weekends. By now I needed to wrap my toe area to protect it from further irritation and pain.

Of course, the pain wasn't as great as it might have been in some people because I have some neuropathy in my feet, which deadens the nerve endings and alleviates a good portion of the discomfort.

I had written a musical composition called **Opus 9/11**, which was a tribute to the courage of the people of New York during the tragedy of 2001. We had scheduled many dates for the performance of this piece. I was feeling the pressure—a mingling of business commitments strongly conflicting with a sense of foreboding concerning the health of my big toe, the region having turned a dark crimson with blisters. I spent hours on the Internet trying to study the condition and had even purchased some liquid silver to use as an antibiotic remedy. At this point, it just didn't seem to me to be something that needed a doctor's attention.

I had never in my life used a doctor as a remedy for an ailment. Or perhaps better stated, I had only used doctors as emergency consultants when all other alternatives had failed. During my traveling years, I had weathered many a physical conflict, coming out seemingly no worse the wear. Why should this be any different? After all, it was just a blistering infection on my big toe.

I spent many hours talking to my wife, Dollie, and my business partner, Janet, about the situation. Each one of us, at varying seasons, gyrated between feeling the need to go to the doctor and really thinking that "today it looks a lot better."

A footnote: I came to a conclusion during this process, that one of the worst things that can happen in our lives is for things to appear to get better without really being resolved. It is the ultimate form of self-deception. For after all, when are we seeing things with the eyes of faith instead of the eyes of reality? And when should the eyes of faith be trusted and the eyes of reality honored?

It was on a Wednesday night, just a few days before the first anniversary of 9/11, following a performance, that I just felt sick. I don't know exactly how to explain it; it was like a sense of ill will, that something was truly wrong, and it was not going to go away with a simple wish and a prayer.

That night, when they unwrapped my foot to check it before bedtime, it looked worse than ever, now showing some blackened skin and cold as ice.

I was scared.

I knew I had to do something quickly. My foot was not getting better. Worse than that, my foot was ceasing to be part of my body, launching into its own tirade of destruction.

I checked myself into the hospital that night. I had so rationalized my situation in an attempt to remain normal that I had failed to notice that two toes were now infected and there was an odor emanating from the wound. After a quick examination, the doctor informed me that I had gangrene in my toes.

I shook my head in disbelief. Gangrene was something that a soldier got at Gettysburg in the Civil War—not some modern-thinking man like myself in the twenty-first century.

They rushed me in for an X-ray to make sure it had not progressed to gas gangrene, which is fatal within hours. Suddenly, I was overwhelmed with the magnitude of my situation. I had taken a simple toe boo-boo to the point of my imminent death. Several emotions pounded me—embarrassment, frustration, incredulity and rage vied for place.

The next morning they informed me that the situation was so serious that my toe would have to be removed. Having grown fond of that toe, I was resistant to the concept. The explained that white flesh and black flesh were both dead flesh, and that my toe was basically gone, but if they amputated, we might be able to keep the infection from spreading up my leg.

They found three different organisms that were infecting my foot. They started me on antibiotics and scheduled surgery. I told them I didn't want to lose my toe, so they agreed to just go in and do a general debridement, cutting away all the dead parts and leaving whatever is living behind.

After that first surgery, I was left with a partial toe and a very dissatisfied surgeon, who warned me that the process had been a waste of time because the toe was going to have to go. I resisted.

I went home and prayed, believing that I would be able to keep the little piece of my little piggy, so I could still take it to market.

But it didn't get better.

I went to another podiatrist, who looked at my foot and then up at me, and said, "Why do you want to keep your toes?"

It seemed like such a foolish question—but apparently my defenses were down. "Because I don't want to lose my toes, and I don't want to be an amputee," I stated bluntly.

He nodded his head and replied, "Well, you're going to be an amputee. The question is whether we're talking about a toe, a foot or a leg."

His choices gave me pause.

Put in these terms, the answer seemed simple. Maybe it was because I was overly attached to my leg, but suddenly my toe didn't seem nearly as important. I agreed.

Unfortunately, the infection had spread to my next toe so the operation would be to remove two toes.

After I returned from surgery, the doctor gingerly removed the bandages, warning me that I would be shocked at what I saw. Honestly, I wasn't. Actually, my foot looked pretty damn good for being minus two toes. They inserted a pick line into my arm, and for six weeks I took a barrage of antibiotics, both orally and intravenously, to counteract the remaining infection.

After six weeks, the infection still lingered, and after taking another culture they discovered they had given me the wrong antibiotics. So I went through another eight-week regimen of more chemicals.

I asked my podiatrist, "What happens if this doesn't work? What drug will you try next?"

He replied, "I don't know. We've pretty well used all the antibiotics there are—A to Z."

I waited for him to chuckle, but not even a smirk. He went in for a third surgery to "polish off the bones," as he called it, to clean up any final infection.

After three operations, nine different antibiotics, and a total of six months, I was adjudged free of infection.

The inactivity imposed during that time put me in horrible shape—I had to relearn how to move and walk. I tried to be productive during the recuperation; writing two new books and two symphonic works, including a musical retrospective on the life of President Kennedy called **Jack**.

I still smile sometimes when I listen to that particular music, because, being zapped by the medications, I have absolutely no memory of writing it nor any of the notes that went into it. So you can either consider it divinely inspired or drug induced.

One night, my friend Janet turned to me and said, "What have you learned from this experience?"

I sat for a long moment. Then I said, "I guess I finally learned a lesson I should have learned in kindergarten. Round pegs go into round holes, pictures look better when you color within the lines, and at the very least, an infected toe can heal quicker if you see a doctor."

Sitting Twenty-Five

Since we are talking about "Digging for Gold in the Rule," I thought it was time to excavate some nuggets. "Do unto others" is rather general in its phrasing. For instance, do *what*?

Well, actually, that's fairly easy. People will pretty well telegraph what they need or want, if you are observant. And if they don't, simply act out in others your own heart's desire. In other words, if you would like a phone call of encouragement, somebody else probably would, too. It is a great place to work from while you're waiting to discern people's messages.

So with that in mind, let's get a little more type specific rather than just speaking in generality about "others."

Do unto mothers and fathers—you will need an adult friend.

Do unto brothers and sisters—your children will cherish a Dutch uncle or an "aunt who will grant."

Do unto your dog—for he will double the devotion in return.

Do unto your cat—it's nice to have something in your life that purrs.

Do unto your boss—everyone needs a favor from someone who has the power to give it.

Do unto your wife—she will give you all the confidence you will ever need.

Do unto your husband—and cajole him into personal growth.

Do unto a tree—and you will have a cool place for shade.

Do unto your car—and it will start on that frosty morning when other cars don't.

Do unto your children—and they will think twice about deceiving you.

Do unto your street person—and they will not need to steal from you.

Do unto your teacher—and they will energize the lesson.

Do unto your preacher—and he will not sink into the doldrums of cynicism.

Do unto your giving—and you will never be without resource when money seems to have abandoned you.

Do unto the planet—and the planet will be instructed to rebuke the devourer.

Do unto God—and He will simplify your path.

Do unto your enemies—and keep them paranoid.

Do unto your body—and your body will bless you with immunity.

Do unto your heart—and you will reap real compassion.

Do unto your mind—and have new ideas appear.

Do unto your friends—and be talked about in a good way behind your back.

Do unto your finance—and money will want to be with you.

Do unto the opposite sex—and you will be astounded by what you have in common.

Do unto your house—and your house will save you from repair bills.

Do unto the stranger—and get him thinking about his own next move.

Do unto the waitress—and get a bigger piece of pie.

Do unto your employees—and watch the productivity increase.

Do unto the air—and feel free to breathe.

Do unto your soul—and watch the fear of death depart.

Do unto religions—and you will find them studying your life.

Do unto the sinner—and the spirit will guide and convict him.

Do unto the outcast—and they will try to find a door into your sanctuary.

and finally,

Do unto the victim—and begin the healing presumed impossible.

Sitting Twenty-Six

My favorite part of any sermon or lecture: "and in conclusion . . ."

Don't you just love to hear those words? Because no matter how interesting a talk may be, it's always good when it's over. Of course, some adept speakers have learned how to insert that phrase, "and in conclusion," several times in their speech, hoping to maintain, or even regain, audience attention. Those are the real sneaky ones who will certainly face their punishment by sitting in some massive hall in eternity watching hours and hours of infomercials.

But, in conclusion (and you can trust me on this one), there is one more "do unto" that needs to be set in motion to improve the ongoing project here on earth.

And it is "do unto yourself, because you know the common perception is coming after you."

The word is *stereotype*. Stereotypes can range from the practical *(fair-skinned people should be careful in the sun)* to the downright bigoted *(people of color are not as smart as white people)*.

Do we have a responsibility to deal with stereotypes, as in what we should do to neutralize them? I know there is a common belief amongst the populace that we should accept each other as we are— "I'm not gonna change for anybody—love me for myself."

But history and holy writings of great men, not to mention just plain common sense, tell us that humankind always looks on the outward appearance, and that it takes a divine spirit to perceive the heart.

If I was dealing with divine thinking, I could relax in my own skin and never be concerned about how I was perceived and therefore received.

But in the noontime heat of daily human interaction, a much more realistic approach is warranted.

Let's be honest, that's why we have family, friends, acquaintances and the rest to surround us all—family is obligated to you, friends have learned to adjust to you, acquaintances will tolerate you to a point, but all the rest of the occupants of this third planet from the sun come to your doorstep with a certain level of expectation and prejudice.

To ignore this is not just naïve, but rather, imperiously arrogant. I am fat. My society tells me that fat people are slow, dull-witted, have no self-control and tend to smell bad. I have two choices. I can spend my life trying to either eliminate or dilute these pre-conceived ideas, or I can make sure that when I'm interacting with people who are not family or friends, I put my personality on a status alert and make sure that I'm not dull-witted, slow, without self-control, and that I always produce an aroma, my finest.

For instance, I think it is foolish to be a black person in the United States of America and go into a restaurant and order fried chicken with a side of watermelon.

It is unfortunate for a woman to display ignorance about business and a dislike for sports in the presence of the male hordes.

And it is spiritually suicidal for Christians to be unaware of what is happening in the world—to be novices about cultural phenomenon.

Stereotypes are an unholy blending of perceived realities and time-tested actual events, which are twisted and contorted, and represented to be the common occurrence.

In other words, because I saw five people in a row do this, an entire race becomes responsible for the action, and also falls victim to how I interpret the action.

You don't need to agree with this, and you can appreciate a lot of things that I've stated in the book without embracing this final point. But let me caution you: public opinion will have its day, and although we certainly do not want to succumb to the pressures of bigotry, we definitely will not kill the ogre by continually feeding the monster.

So how can you "do unto yourself?" The human journey is a concerted effort to present to others the personal resume that we want them to read about ourselves. As much as possible, we want to avoid allowing the weaker fellows in our communities to focus on tiny details and blow them out of proportion to create glaring revelations. It is a personal choice, one you must make for yourself.

So arm yourself. Learn what stereotype the present mental drone of society has inflicted upon you.

Do I want to continue to perpetuate the idea that I am an entity unto myself, subordinate to no one else, and therefore am able to select whatever mannerism or profile I desire? Or am I a student of this planet? A fellow-journeyman with other humans, many the same, some stronger and others weaker, to whom I should be sensitive and not tempt to fall into ignorant realms of judgment simply because my repeated behavior within their eyesight or earshot thrusts a stereotype to the front of their minds?

DUO—Do Unto Others—is the ultimate act of intelligence—mercy rallying to the situations of the feeble commonality of everyday thinking.

We can make a difference. If we wait to do it from a seat of power, that power will have to be absolute and therefore inevitably corrupted. Choosing to make a difference from a position of service is climbing inside your own soul, finding your dreams, looking for a practical way of expressing them and then just going out and doing it—hell to pay.

Jonathan Richard Cring

Jonathan Richard Cring is the composer of ten symphonies, the author of eight books, including **I'M . . . the legend of the son of man, Liary, Holy Peace . . . the story of Iz and Pal, Jesonian, Preparing a Place and Digging for Gold.** His thirty-year experience has taken him from the grease paint of theater to a time as an evangelist among the gospel saints. He is the winner of a Billboard Music Award and is the in-house composer for the Sumner County Symphony. He travels the country lecturing as an advocate for the Jesonian movement. He has been married for thirty-four years and is the father of three sons and guardian to three others. He lives in Hendersonville, Tennessee.

Also from the Author

Finding the Lily (to consider)
A journette of the journey.

When I was a kid they didn't have Big Men's Stores - at
least, none my parents told me about. So my mother would buy
me the only pants she could find in my size - work pants.

Dickie work pants. For some reason, she would choose the
green ones - the color created by smashing a bag of green peas
into a frog. And speaking of being smashed, for some reason,
she wouldn't buy them my size, I guess because she didn't want
to admit how big I was. And so she would purchase them so
small that I would have to suck in to button them. That's what
you like when you're fat. Tight green clothes. Of course, these
pants were so stiff they could stand by themselves, which I have
to admit, came in handy when waiting in line at an amusement
park.

Preparing a Place [for myself]

The perfect book for all those folks who would like to die just long enough to find out what the crap is going on – then come back to pizza. I always wanted to meet God. When I was a child, very small, I thought he would look like Reverend Bacorra, a Presbyterian minister I knew- salt and pepper hair, tall, glasses, donning a black robe, wearing oxblood, shiny shoes with scuffed tips.

As I grew older my image changed, but always, I envisioned a physical presence – an actual being. Now, where was God?

I wondered if God was merely light, love and spirit. I smiled at my own ramblings. Light, love and spirit - not a bad triangle.

Still, I wanted to meet God, fact to face, as it were. a bad triangle.

Still, I wanted to meet God, fact to face, as it were.

Holy Peace. .. the story of Iz and Pal

In a basket full of oranges, it is always the singular apple that gains our attention. This is a wonderful characteristic of the human soul. So in our day and age, in the midst of clamoring for resolutions based on military might, a breath of fresh air comes in to the atmosphere of pending war. Amir and Jubal – two boys who grew up on different sides of the tracks of a conflict – one Arab, one Jew. They rename themselves Iz and Pal and determine to maintain their friendship amidst the granite – headed thinking of their friendship amidst the granite-headed thinking of their society. Where their journey takes them, the friends they make along the way, the surprising enemies, and the stunning resolution, will keep you riveted to the brief pages of this odyssey into peace.

Jonathan *by* I'M... *the legend of the son of man*

A novel on the life of Jesus Christ focusing on his humanity, passion, and personality—highlighting struggles with his family, sexuality, abduction by zealots, humor and wit, and interaction with characters bound by tradition, affection, legalism, politics, and religious fanaticism—congealed into a 416 page entertaining and inspirational quick read; non-theological and mind enriching.

Jesonian
A decision to take spirituality personally.

Stagnancy is the decision to settle for less than we know we need. In every generation, there must be a voice reminding us of our true mission, prodding us on to escape mediocrity and stirring the waters to freshen the stream of thinking. Jesonian is a book that poses the questions in the heart of every human who seeks to find some nourishment for his hardening soul – every man, woman and child who yearns for a message with meaning and wants to escape the rigors of religion and find the true spirit in spirituality.

Printed in the United States
216139BV00001B/8/A

9 780970 436177